Art Of Conversation
Easy To Learn

Ram Nivas Kumar

MA (English), MLISc., MJMC, Dip-in-OA

ISBN

Edition
2024
Copyright
Ram Nivas Kumar
Published by
Ram Nivas Kumar
Page Setup
Printed at
Price

PREFACE

Knowledge of English is regarded as an index of education and the ability to speak English correctly is regarded as an index of good schooling. Without knowledge of English, the education of a literate person may seem to be interrogated. Now, learning English is an ever-growing demand. And, to speak English correctly is a social requirement as well.

Being a medium of international communication, the ability of speaking English is much more necessary. The liberalization of Indian economy and globalization of trade and business have brought about a situation where speaking English correctly has increased. Hence, we have the presentation of this book. It is meant for students and professionals having general learning of English who are unable to speak so well. Our motto is to spread learning of spoken English among non-native speakers. Hope, we will succeed doing so.

The book contains forty units. The first ten units are meant for junior students. The rest are designed for higher ups. Some deal with functions and some other with conversations. Some are followed by most useful expressions that can be used on different occasions.

Students and other readers are suggested to make a good practice of each sentence. Just read and repeat. Read aloud. Your tongue and mind will get a twist to English tone. It will help you speak so well. Just do this as often as possible until the expressions are fully internalized.

Hope, you will find this book a guide to your requirement.
-Ram Nivas Kumar

CONTENTS

Importance of Good Conversation

IMPORTANCE OF GOOD CONVERSATION

In our day-to-day life, what we need first is good conversation. The art of good conversation can be developed by learning a little and practicing it much. Conversation is a fine art. It is the art of exchanging thoughts. It is an art which even the least educated person can learn. Not everybody can paint or play music, but almost everyone can talk.

Conversation, therefore, is an art so important that gives the greatest pleasure to all of us. "To talk is our chief business in the world. Talk is by far the greatest source of pleasure. It costs nothing in money. It is all profit. It completes our education. It maintains our friendship. It can be enjoyed at any age and in almost every state of health."–says R L Stevenson.

Conversation is indeed the most easily teachable of all the arts. All you need to do in order to become a good talker is to find a subject that interests you and your listener. There are, for example, numberless hobbies to talk about. But the important thing is that you must talk about the other fellow's hobby rather than your own. Therein lies the secret of your popularity. Talk to your friends about the things that interest them. You will get a name for good fellowship, charming wit and a brilliant mind. There is nothing that pleases people so much as your interest in their subjects.

It is just as important to know what subjects to avoid and what subjects to select for good conversation. If you don't want to be a bore, be careful to avoid certain unpleasant topics. Avoid talking about yourself unless you are asked to do so. People are interested in their own problems, not in yours. So take care of all these things.

Just pick a topic. Make much practice on it. Take a turn

to next one. Go on doing like this. And evolve the art of good conversation hidden in you.

1. CONVERSATION ABOUT A SCHOOL

(Aman is asking Shahid about his school. See how the conversation goes.)

Aman : Hello, friend! What's your name?

Shahid : My name is Shahid.

Aman : What school do you read in?

Shahid : I read in V.S. Primary School.

Aman : What is the full name of your school?

Shahid : It is Vidya Sagar Primary School.

Aman : Where is it situated?

Shahid : It is situated at Salalpur in Nalanda District.

Aman : Is it a big school?

Shahid : No, it is a small school.

Aman : How many students are there in your school?

Shahid : There are one hundred students in our school.

Aman : How many teachers are there?

Shahid : There are seven teachers in this school.

Aman : How many class rooms are there?

Shahid : There are five class rooms.

Aman : Is there a playground in front of your school?

Shahid : Yes, there is a playground in front of my school.

Aman : Is there any potable water facility in your school?

Shahid : Yes, there is potable water facility in my school.

Aman : Who is the class teacher?

Shahid : Shri B.C. Pathak is the class teacher.

Aman : Who is the Head Master of your school?

Shahid : Md. Zafar Aalam is the Head Master of my school.

Aman : Who is your best friend?

Shahid : Rohit is my best friend.

Aman : What time does your school start?
Shahid : My school starts at 8.30 in the morning.
Aman : What colour is the building of the school?
Shahid : The colour of my school building is yellow.
Aman : How far is your school from your house?
Shahid : Not very far. It is half a kilometre.
Aman : Do you go to your school on rickshaw or on foot?
Shahid : I go to my school on foot.
Aman : Do you like your school?
Shahid : Yes, I like my school very much.
Aman : It was nice talking to you.
Shahid : Thank you.

2. CONVERSATION IN THE WAITING HALL

(Saniya along with her mother is talking to the receptionist in school waiting hall. See how they talk.)

Mother : Good morning, sir.

Receptionist Good morning, madam.

Mother : I want admission of my daughter to this school. So we have come here.

Receptionist: OK, madam. You are welcome. Just wait for a while in the waiting hall. The Head Mistress might be coming.

Saniya : Is this a children school?

Receptionist Yes, this is a children school.

Saniya : How many students are there?

Receptionist There are four hundred students.

Saniya : Who is the class teacher of class III?

Receptionist Mrs. Madona is the class teacher of class III.

Saniya : Does she beat the students?

Receptionist No, she never beats. She ever loves all.

Saniya : Who is the Principal of this school?

Receptionist Smt. Vandana Gupta is the Head Mistress of this school.

Saniya : Is there any sports facility available in this school?

Receptionist Yes, there are several sports facilities available here.

Saniya : Is there a playground to play in?

Receptionist Of course. There is a big playground.

Saniya : Is there a garden?

Receptionist Yes, there is a garden. You may visit it.

Saniya : Very good. I love this school. Mom, get me admitted to this school.

Mother : Surely. I too like this school.

3. WITH THE HEAD MISTRESS
(Saniya along with her mother is going to the Head Mistress. See how she talks.)
Student 1 : Where are you going?
Saniya : I am going to the Head Mistress.
Student 1 : Why are you going to the Head Mistress?
Saniya : I have to meet her.
Student 1 : But why? What is the work?
Saniya : I have to take admission to class III.
Student 1 : Yeah, good idea, you must go.
Saniya : May I come in, madam?
Head Mistress Of course, you may come in.
Saniya : Good morning, madam. Well, I have to take

admission to this school.

Head Mistress To what class?
Saniya : To class III.
Head Mistress What is your name?
Saniya : I am Saniya, madam.
Head Mistress What class did you pass?
Saniya : I have passed class II.
Head Mistress How many chairs are there, Saniya?
Saniya : There are four chairs, madam.
Head Mistress Which school did you study in?
Saniya : I studied in Vidya Sagar Primary School, Salalpur.
Head Mistress Where is it located?
Saniya : It is located at village Salalpur under Parwalpur block

in Nalanda District.

Head Mistress What does your father do?
Saniya : He is a businessman.

Head Mistress Who is there with you?
Saniya : She is my mother.
Head Mistress You are a good student.
Saniya : Thank you, madam.

4. WITH THE CLASS TEACHER

(A new student comes to his school for the first time. He meets his class teacher.)

Piyush : May I come in, sir?

Class Teacher Yes, you may come in.

Piyush : Sir, I am a new student. I've came to see you.

Class Teacher What's your name?

Piyush : It is Piyush, sir.

Class Teacher Which class do you read in?

Piyush : I read in class III, sir.

Class Teacher What is your father's name?

Piyush : My father's name is Shri Kamlakant Sahay.

Class Teacher Where do you live?

Piyush : I live at Nishchalganj under Parwalpur police station.

Class Teacher Did you come in an auto-rickshaw or by bicycle?

Piyush : I came in an auto-rickshaw, sir.

Class Teacher What do you expect from me?

Piyush : Your love, caring and learning, sir.

Class Teacher You are a good student. I extend you my warm love

and affection.

Piyush : Thank you, sir.

5. IN THE CLASS ROOM

(Two students are talking together in the class room. See how they talk.)

Student1 : Ours is a very big class room.

Student2 : You are right. It is very big.

Student 1 : It has four fans.

Student 2 : But one fan is not working.

Student 1 : I see, there must be some problem.

Student2 : Its blackboard is also very large.

Student 1 : Look at the date written in the corner. It is 1stApril, 2021.

Student 2 : There are twenty benches to sit on.

Student 1 : And there is also a chair for the teacher.

Student 2 How nice is the doormat!

Student 1 : Very nice. It is new and pretty.

Student 2 : The four walls are painted well.

Student 1 : And what do you think of our class teacher?

Student 2 : She is very smart, intelligent and labourious.

Student 1 : What subjects does she teach?

Student 2 : She teaches us English and Science.

Student 1 : What is the real time of recess?

Student2 : It is exactly at 01.00 pm.

Student1 : Does our school open at 10.15 or 10.30?

Student 2 : Our school opens at 10.30 am.

Student 1 : It means we have to reach our school at 10.15am.

Student 2 : Yes, you are right.

Student 1 : Is there any music teacher in this school?

Student 2 : Yes, there is a music teacher. She is Ms. Monika.

Student 1 : Have you seen the school library?

Student 2 : Yes, I have seen the library. It is very attractive.

Student 1 : Have you visited the school canteen?

Student 2 : Yes, I visited it only yesterday and ate there two rasogullas.

Student 1 : Have you seen the rose garden?
Student2 : No, I have not. Let's visit it in the recess.
Student 1 : OK, we shall visit it.

6. IN THE LIBRARY

(Misha is talking with Librarian. See how they talk.)

Misha : Good morning, sir.

Librarian : Good morning, Misha. How are you?

Misha : Fine. Thanks. And you, sir?

Librarian : Very well.

Misha : Sir, this is a good library.

Librarian : Of course, this is very useful as well.

Misha : How many books are there?

Librarian : There are two thousand books available here.

Misha : Is there any book on comics?

Librarian : No, comic books are not allowed.

Misha : No matter. I need a book on essays.

Librarian : Sure. This is an essay book.

Misha : May I borrow it now?

Librarian Yes, you may borrow it.

Misha : When do I have to return this?

Librarian : You have to return this within fifteen days.

Misha : Surely, I will return it in time. May I take another book, sir?

Librarian : You may take two books at a time.

Misha : Give me that book on Dr. Rajendra Prasad by R N Kumar.

Librarian : Surely. Take it. But let me note it on your library ticket.

Misha : Thank you, sir.

7. AT THE FEE COUNTER

(Shami along with his mother is talking to a fee clerk at the fee counter of his school. Learn how they talk.)

Shami : Good morning, sir.

Clerk : Good morning, Shami. Tell me your work.

Shami : Sir, I have to pay the fee.

Clerk : Of course, you may pay the fee.

Shami : How much amount is due, sir?

Clerk : Your fee is due for three months. It stands for Rs. 300/-.

Shami : Actually, my dad was away. So, he could not pay.

Clerk : Fee for one month is Rs. 100/- and for three months, it stands at Rs. 300/-.

Shami : What is the period it is due for, sir?

Clerk : It is due for May, June and July, 2021.

Shami : Mammy, give me the money. Fee is due for three months. It stands at Rs 300/-.

Mother : Take it and go to the counter. Pay it right this time. I will wait for you here.

Shami : Take this amount, sir.

Clerk : Wait for a moment. I will give you the receipt...Take this and keep it safe on leaving the counter. Give it to your

mother soon.

Shami : OK, sir. Thank you.

8. IN THE EXAMINATION HALL

(Two students- Monita and Parul are talking in the school test hall.
Learn how they talk.)

Monita : Is this the examination hall?

Parul : Yes, this is the examination hall.

Monita : I think our examination will be held in this hall.

Parul : No, our class test is not in this hall.

Monita : Then, where is our hall?

Parul : Our test is in room No. 2.

Monita : Let's go to our hall.

Monita : Is this our test hall?

Parul : Yes, it is.

Monita : What time does our test start?

Parul : It starts at 8.30 am.

Monita : The time is up. Our class teacher has not yet come.

Parul She might be coming...Lo! She has come.

Monita : May I go out for a while?

Class Teacher Yes, you may go but come soon.

Monita : My pencil does not write well. Could you please spare
one for me?

Parul : Surely, you may take this.

Monita : Do you have an eraser?

Parul : Yes, I have.

Monita : Could you please give it for a while?

Parul : Of course. Take it but return it soon.

Monita : Today is the Maths test, isn't it?

Parul : No, Maths test is not today. It is science test today.

Monita : It means the programme has changed.

Parul : Yes, you're right.
Monita : Now the time starts for the test.
Parul : Let's stop talking and be ready for the test.

9. IN THE CANTEEN

(Two friends Samir and Nadim are talking to the school canteen staff.
See how they talk.)

Samir : Let's go to the canteen for the juice.

Nadim : Let's, but I will not take juice. I'll eat some sweets.

Samir : OK. As you like.

(In the Canteen)

Nadim : Uncle, give me a piece of milk-cake.

Staff ; Surely... Take this. It is quite fresh. It has been

prepared right this day.

Samir : A cup of mango juice, please.

Staff : Just serving... This one. This is prepared from good
quality of mango.

Samir : It's very tasty. But quantity of milk is a little less.
Please add some milk to it.

Staff : Just carrying... Take it.

Samir : You prepare good drinks for us. Thank you, uncle.

Nadim : How much is this rasogulla?

Staff : Five rupees a piece.

Nadim : Give me a piece of rasogulla also.

Staff : Surely...This one. This is quite fresh.

Samir : What's the price for my juice?

Staff : It is fifteen rupees.

Samir : Take this money.

Nadim : And what is the price for my milk-cake and rasogulla?

Staff : It is nine rupees only.

Nadim : Please note it in my diary. I have no money on me

now. I shall pay you tomorrow.

Staff : OK. Thanks a lot.

10. IN THE PLAYGROUND

(Some boys are playing in the field. Learn how they talk.)

Aarush : It is play time now. Let's go to play.

Faiz : What game shall we play today?

Aarush : We shall play football today.

Paawan : Good idea. Just take out the ball.

Bailey : I shall be the goal-keeper.

Paawan : Yes, you will.

Bailey : I shall start the game by kicking the ball hard.

Aarush : Our game teacher is also coming.

Faiz : We should wait for him.

Aarush : He is our guide.

Paawan : The ball has come.

Faiz : But this ball is too big.

Bailey : You can change it by a smaller one.

Paawan : Yes, we may change it.

Aarush : This ball is a smaller one.

All boys : We should start the game now.

(The game teacher whistles off and the game starts.)

Bailey : Half an hour has passed. We should stop the game

now.

Faiz : But the game period is of forty minutes.

Teacher : Stop playing. The time is over.

All boys : Yes, sir. We should stop playing.

Teacher : Go to your class-room.

All boys : Yes, sir. We are going.

Arush : It was a very interesting match.

RAM NIVAS KUMAR

Faiz : Yes, you are right. It gave us much pleasure.

11. TWO FRIENDS TALKING

Aman : Is your Roll No. 212?

Dipu : Yes, it is.

Aman : What is your name?

Dipu: My name is Ravi Shanker Prasad.

Aman : Where do you live?

Dipu : I live in a village.

Aman: How far is your village from this town?

Dipu : It is at a distance of four miles from here.

Aman : How do you go to your college?

Dipu : I walk the distance without much difficulty.

Aman : Don't you have a bicycle?

Dipu : No, I don't. Even if I had one, I would prefer walking to riding on a bicycle.

Aman : Why?

Dipu : What about the city-dwellers?

Aman : They're ease loving, aren't they? But they've their own share of trouble. They struggle hard, don't they?

Dipu : I beg to differ with you. They've more of comfort. They whistle away their time.

Aman : And what do you people do?

Dipu : We struggle against the vagaries of Nature. For us,

life is no merry note; it is a painful drag.

Aman : You're partly true, aren't you?

Dipu : Let's then agree to differ.

12. ADMISSION TO A SCHOOL

(A mother along with her daughter visits an English medium School for admission. See how she gets her daughter admitted in that school.)

Mother : Good morning, madam.

Receptionist: Good morning.

Mother : We have come for my daughter's admission

to this school. Could you please help me?

Receptionist: Yes, of course. There's a procedure. You first

have to fill up the registration form. Just go
to that desk.

Mother : Well, I have to get a registration form for
admission of my daughter.

Clerk : To which class?

Mother : She has passed class IV and has to seek

admission to class V.

Clerk : OK. Just fill up this form. She will have to sit
for a test. And the admission test is scheduled
to be held right tomorrow exactly at 11.30
am. So come on time and let her attend the
test.

(The next day the daughter, Monita, attends the test and fails.)

Mother : My daughter, Monita, has not qualified the

test. She could not understand the questions

well. Hence, was unable to write answers in full. But we are
sure, she will catch up soon.

In-Charge : I cannot render any help. Just meet our

Principal. He may extend you a grace and
allow your admission.

(Mother goes to the Principal and urges for admission.)
Mother : Good morning, sir. We have come to seek

your grace.

Principal : Good morning. Tell me what's the problem.
Mother : Monita could not qualify the admission test.

She is unable to get admission to your
school. Her Maths and Science are good.
English is a little poor. But she will pick up soon.

Principal : Don't worry. We will take personal care of

hers. Her admission is allowed. Take admission today itself.

Mother : Thank you, sir.

13. MOVIE AT SCHOOL AUDITORIUM

(Manik meets his friend Tapan and suggests that they should go to a movie.)

Manik : Hello, Tapan !

Tapan : Hi Manik! Glad to see you after so many days.

Manik : I've been away for a few days. What're your plans for

the coming Sunday?

Tapan : Nothing in particular.

Manik : Why? Do you know there's going to be a show of

children's film at school auditorium.

Tapan : Yes, I've heard that. But...

Manik : How about going to the movie this Sunday? It's going

to be shown at school auditorium itself.

Tapan : OK. Good idea. What film is it?

Manik : It's *Mighty Raju*, an animated film based on the

power and science.

Tapan : Yes, we will go and enjoy.

Manik : Then, when and where to meet?

Tapan : It'd be better, if we meet at 2.00 pm at the main gate

of the auditorium.

Manik : OK. All good. We'll meet and enjoy.

Tapan : Fine, I'll be there.

Manik : See you at 2.00 pm then.

Tapan : See you.

14. PLANNING FOR THE 1st JANUARY

(Two friends are talking about the upcoming new year, 2022. See how they talk.)

Marlow : The new year, 2022 is round the corner.

Hasting : Yes, you're right. The year 2021 is in its last gasp.

Marlow : Each year brings in its train new hopes. We welcome it with a new determination.

Hasting : Surely, we will do it this year also.

Marlow : We learn from the experience. We try not to repeat the past mistakes.

Hasting : Yeah, we draw up new plans with renewed vigour. What do you think?

Marlow : We should think about the task of translating them into a reality.

Hasting : You're right. I'll prepare the balance sheet of failures and achievements and will do accordingly. Tell me your opinion.

Marlow : In each year, the same story of the old year is repeated. I've hopes belied. Also, I have the dreams shattered. And the same is again on continuation with me. So, nothing new comes up.

Hasting : Let's look forward to the advent of the new year, 2022 and

plan to do something new and novel for the welfare of our society.

Marlow : OK, great idea. We should first find time to worship God

and not to party for making merry. This is my planning for the first January next year.

Hasting : Yours is a nice idea. Some of my friends planned for Bodh-Gaya and asked me to accompany them on the 1st January, 2022. But I denied. Mine is not a thought like this. *Karma* is bigger and better than thinking of rejoicing it. And for doing good *Karma,* we should first move towards God. He will provide power. Enjoyment comes thereafter.

Marlow : Let's agree to one thought. We're really fast friends and will continue till last march.

15. A BIRTHDAY PARTY

(Some children of the same locality enjoy a party of Lima's birthday.
Note how they make merry.)

Lima : Hi, Chikoo! Today's my birthday. I invite you to attend my
party

at 7.00 pm. I've invited several other friends.

Chikoo : Nice. I will surely attend it. I will also bring some of your
friends with me.

Lima : Thank you.

Lima : Mammy, I have invited ten friends in total. Prepare the cake

and do the needful.

Mammy : Your cake is ready for use. Decorate it and arrange the
table.

Lima : I have to bring some decorative items. Please give me some
money.

Mammy : Take it from the purse. Accompany any of your friends.

And go to the Bristle Stores. That's a good shopping point.

You may find all decorative items there at a cheap rate. The
salesman is well-mannered and deals in a pleasing behaviour.
Your dad always makes his purchases from that shop.

Lima : Good idea, mom. We will do so.

(At 7.00 pm, invitees reach the house of Lima.)

Nikoo : Happy birthday, Lima.

Lima : Thank you.

Nikoo : Here's a small gift for you.

Lima : Oh! There's no need... But this is how you feel. A token of
love and affection as well. So, I have to accept it.

Mikoo : Birthday congratulations !
Lima : Thank you dear friend. Just come in. Take a piece of cake,

one balloon also. Eat sweets and talk to my mom and dad.
They are very fond of you. They often talk of you.

Mikoo : Nice to hear. We all regard them and in turn they exchange
their love.
Nikoo : Let's all take a leave. It's getting late. Mom would worry if I
am late. Bye Lima!
Lima : Bye!

16. A MARRIAGE CEREMONY

(Kamal's marriage is fixed. Baraat is on 19th of this month. See how everything goes in his marriage party.)
Father : Raman Babu has an educated family. His daughter, Divya, is beautiful. She is very practical; bears noble look as well. Why don't you think of her for Kamal?

Mother : I too think that she will be a perfect match for Kamal.
Priest : Yajman, it is difficult to find a proper match these days.

Don't go on thinking so much. Just accept the proposal. Send them your 'Haan.' 19th May is a pious day. Invitation should be sent out and all arrangements to be made well in advance.

Kamal : Friends, my marriage is settled. It is on the 19th of this

month. Please accept my invitation to attend all functions.

Friend : Glad to know this. Surely... Will attend and enjoy.
(Baraat moves for Birampur with a host of 100 noble people.)
Peter : What an attractive scene! There are full preparations. It's all A charming scenario. Several counters with delicious foods awaiting us. Let's enjoy first.
Jitan : Yes, we must. There's a dance programme also. After we have our food, we will go for the dance party and enjoy.
Peter : Yeah. Good idea.

Jitan : Just call for Kamal also. We would make a dance recording.

It would be a nice occasion. Kamal dances well in Bhangra. He was such a miracle in my wedding.

Peter : He has already gone on Mandap. Let'send the programme and move for dinner. People have already started.
Jitan : OK. Must move... Well, the foods have been prepared with much care. Sweets are delicious.
Peter : You are right. The girl's parents might have spent a lot. They seem to have taken much care of taste and quality. Thanks to them.
Jitan : Would it be better to stay or return right now?
Peter : Well, it is 10 pm only. Better to take leave and be back

home. My mother would be sleepless. She will be happy to see me.

Jitan : Good suggestion. Let's be on our way back home. It was a

grand reception.

Peter : Bye Jitan!
Jitan : Bye!

17. CLEANLINESS CAMPAIGN

Richa : What's the meeting for?

Nidhi : They are organizing a cleanliness campaign in our locality.

Richa : What is it about?

Nidhi : This is a nice nation-wide programme launched by our honourable Prime Minister on 2nd October, 2014.

Richa : What is the purposes of all this?

Nidhi : The aim of this initiative is to create social awareness to clean the country.

Richa : People should be aware of the need to maintain environmental cleanliness. It is very essential to us.

Nidhi : Yes, cleanliness is next to godliness. We must maintain it.

Aashiya : It brings progress and improvement in all spheres of life.

Richa : I also want to join the campaign.

Nidhi : Yes, we all will be joining this.

Aashiya : Meet me at 10 am tomorrow. We will be out with a broom

and a basket for cleaning the streets. We will start from the

house of Dr. Rahman and will go up to Peter Anderson. We

will also raise consciousness among the street dwellers. They may help us keep our colony neat and clean.

Nidhi : Surely, we will do so. We will join with some more friends.

Aashiya : Bye for now.

18. VISIT TO AN SP

(Mihir writes a letter to the Superintendent of Police and seeks his permission to see him. On permission so granted, he visits the SP. See how they converse.)

SP : Amit Kumar, SP of this city, speaking here.

Mihir : Good afternoon, sir.

SP : Well, have you written a letter to us?

Mihir : Yes, sir. I've written one. A week ago. I want to see you.

Could you please permit me?

SP : Of course, you are free to meet me. No need to seek specific permission. You may come this evening at 4 O'clock.

Mihir It is pleasing to hear this. Coming soon, sir.

(Mihir is going to the SP to meet him.)

Mihir : Good evening, sir.

SP : Good evening, Mihir.

Mihir : Well, I wanted to see you. So I wrote you the letter.

SP : OK. We received your letter today itself. And decided to call

you up.

Mihir : Thank you, sir.

SP : Mihir! You have written that you are a student of class VIII.

But your writing seems to be of a student of class X. I read your letter time and again. It makes me very happy.

Mihir : My mammy is a teacher. She guides me in a different way.

SP : OK. What does your father do?

Mihir : My father is a small farmer. He works in the field.

ART OF CONVERSATION: EASY TO LEARN

SP : Which school do you read in?

Mihir : I read in Manas Chetan School in my village, sir.

SP : Good, very good. Tell me what do you want to be in life?

Mihir : I want to serve the people by becoming a police officer.

SP : OK. Then you have to be very honest and sincere. You have

  to labour hard right from this time.

Mihir : Surely, sir. I'll follow.

SP : Whenever you need any help, feel free to contact me. My good wishes to you for your bright future.

Mihir : Thank you, sir. Good night.

19. VISIT TO THE DM

(Some intellectuals visit District Magistrate to discuss local problems and find their solutions. Learn how they talk to the DM and resolve their problems.)

Representative : Good afternoon, sir.

DM : Good afternoon.

Representative: We are residents of Durgapuri under

Malighat Mohalla. We are facing a lot of problems for years. During rainy season, there is water logging at several places.

DM : We are abreast of it. We are in touch with municipal authority. We have ordered them

to fill up the small ditches at once. They are doing their work.

Representative: Road soling is another work to be done.

DM : Proposals have been approved. We have

asked the Executive Engineer to prepare the estimate. As soon as it comes before me, we will try to get the work done. This work requires ministerial approval as well. But we will do this quickly. Our government is taking all measures for the welfare

of the public.

Representative: Thank you, sir. Well, we are peace-loving

citizens. We take care of our locality. Now-a-days we notice that some miscreants often hobnob our location. They are outsiders. They comment absurdly on street girls and even speak abusive words. This hurts our feeling. Some parents are scared. We request you to take a note of it and bring them round the fold of law.

DM : Surely, if there's anything like this. We

would certainly punish them. This is our main duty to see that no one harms anybody in any way.

Representative: Thank you, sir. Regards to your majesty. You

are the District Magistrate and Collector who

has got vast power. We know- a DM can go even beyond the written boundary of law in the state of crisis, emergency and exigency. We are proud of you.

DM : Thank you.
Representative: Thanks, sir. It was nice to see you.

20. COMPLAINT AGAINST AN OFFICIAL

(A Revenue Clerk is harassing a member of public named Udit for bribe in connection with mutation of land. See how he makes a complaint against the corrupt official and brings him round the fold of law.)

Udit : Good morning, sir. I am Udit. I have purchased a

chunk of land in municipal area. Here's the registry paper. I want its mutation. Please do the work.

R. Clerk : No mutation work is on these days. Come again next week.

Udit : But why? Your office is open. All government

work is going on. Why should I come next week?

R. Clerk : I can simply say that we are not doing any mutation work.
Udit : But what are you doing these days? Well, you are a revenue clerk. You are meant for this work. You

can't deny this work.

R. Clerk : Don't teach me my work. You are not to supervise

me.

Udit : I am not to supervise. Surely not... But I can surely

get this work done by you, or otherwise I am free to

complain against you and your work attitude.

(Udit writes a complaint and proceeds to the Circle Officer.)
Udit : Sir, your revenue clerk does not accept my work

relating to mutation. He is harassing for a long time.

He says- "Mutation work is not going on these days".He even

does not behave well. He shows ill intention for illegal gratification. I can't bear with it.

CO : That's not good. He can't deny the work. He has to

do this. Give me all the papers. Your work will be completed. Mutation work takes time. Come again after forty days. Meanwhile, we will enquire into the matter and deal with him departmentally. Rules are there. So, don't get disheartened.

Udit : Thank you, sir. Such type of official must be

punished who takes pleasure in vexing general public and asks for any ransom. I request you to go through the matter in detail and punish him so that no one can dare to harass anybody in future.

CO : We will surely do so. Keep it a belief in rules of

law.

Udit : Thank you, sir.

21. SETTLING A QUARREL

(Shyam Babu along with Madhavan is out in the locality. They see some students quarrelling. See how they deal with and settle the quarrel.)
Shyam Babu : What's the crowd for?
Madhavan : It seems some students are fighting.
Shyam Babu : But why and for what?
Madhavan : They're students of our own locality, seem to be

fighting with their own friends.

Shyam Babu : Lo! One began to beat the other. Hello, Madhavan!

just follow me. Let's see who are they and what's the

matter.
Madhavan : Yeah, we must... Well, one is the son of Dr. Tiwari

and the other, the son of Prof. Imaran. Both are of our locality.

Shyam Babu : What are you quarrelling for? Well, you're intelligent students. It is not good to behave like this.
Diwakar : Namaste, uncle. Well, we were coming from

our school. Rohan pushed me down on the road. He's very wicked. He often uses ill words. So, I objected him.

Shyam Babu: Rohan, it's very bad to push on the road.

Rohan : Sorry, uncle. Well, my friend Diwakar always teases

me. He vexed me this time again. So, I pushed him
and he fell down.

Madhavan : But you can't behave like this. It's very bad. It may

hurt him severely. So why don't you think next time?

Rohan : Sorry, uncle.

Shyam Babu: Rohan, you're dear to me. I always love you. Won't you please...?

Rohan : I'm very sorry, Uncle.
Shyam Babu: Well, you are of same locality. Your parents are respectable people. And you're intelligent students.
We're proud of you. It doesn't behove you.
Rohan : Sorry, uncle. I'm very sorry for this. I'll not do this

again. I realize my fault.

Diwakar : I'm ashamed too. I'll never tease him. I shake hands

with my friend.

Rohan : I promise not to do this again. I will live up to the high expectation.
Shyam Babu: Good, nice to listen from you.
Students : Regards to you all.
Shyam Babu : Thanks.

22. AT THE POLICE STATION

(Last night some dacoits attacked the house of Mr. Babbar. In the morning, he goes to the police station for lodging an FIR. See how he deals with the police officer.)

Mr. Babbar : Very bad, sir. Very bad.

P. Officer : What happened? Why do you seem so

nervous?

Mr. Babbar : There's a dacoity, huzoor. It occurred last

night. Fortunately, we all are safe. It

happened at midnight. They may be twenty

in number.They surrounded the house all of a sudden. Fired closely. Even hurled some bombs at the windows. We had to hide ourselves to save our lives. The dacoits broke open the door and entered the house. Captured us and looted away everything.

P. Officer : Have they left any of their own things at the

site?

Mr. Babbar : Yes, sir. They have left a big iron rod, a

towel and a pair of shoes.

P. Officer : Okay. We take a serious note of the

incidence. We will reach the spot within an hour. You need not fear any more. The police are with you. Have faith in law. Well, did you recognize any of them?

Mr. Babbar : No sir. All were unknown people. They were

equipped with arms and ammunition. And were bearing masks to hide their identity.

P. Officer : Don't be nervous. We will soon arrest all of

them and put into jail. Tell us what are the goods looted from the house?

Mr. Babbar : Here's the list, sir. Belongings were of high

cost of about Rs. ten lakh.

P. Officer : It is a big dacoity. We take a serious note of

it; register the case and put it in motion. We are sure to arrest the dacoits and recover the booty within a week. You may go now.

Mr. Babbar : Thank you, sir. Hope, you would bring

our expectation at par.

23. ADMISSION TO HOSPITAL

(Mahendra has fallen from chair and has broken his waist bone. He is crying with pain. He is carried to hospital for treatment.)

Birendra : Very bad. Well, Mahendra has fallen from chair

and is badly injured. He is crying for help.

Jitendra : O my God! How did it all happen?

Birendra : At night, the electric bulb had fused. He wanted to change it with a new one. So, he stood up on a

plastic chair. But the chair ringed and he fell down. He has severe pain in his waist.

Jitendra : Just call for a vehicle. Call for some more friends. We have to carry him to hospital immediately.

Birendra : The vehicle has just arrived. Let's carry the patient properly into the vehicle.
(They carried the patient to hospital.)
Birendra : Where is the emergency ward?
Attendant : Take this ticket and go to that counter.
Birendra : Emergency service, please. My friend has perhaps

broken his waist bone. Pain is unbearable. Please do hurry.

Hospital I/C: Your duty is over. Please put the patient over to

me. We must do what's needed.

Birendra : Thank you.
Doctor : Lay down the patient. Let me check him up... He has got a minor fracture. Don't worry.

Nothing serious. It needs a plaster. I have

prescribed some medicine. Give it to the patient regularly. Come again after forty days.

Birendra : Can we take the patient home now?
Doctor : No, not right now. First, get a discharge slip from

the hospital clerk and take the patient in the afternoon.

Birendra : Thank you, doctor.

24. DREADFUL SCENE IN A HOSPITAL

(Two villagers are in the Patna General Hospital. They talk to each other at the scene in the hospital. Let's see how they talk.)

Villager 1 : This is Patna General Hospital. Just look at it.

Villager 2 : Oh! It presents a dreadful scene. I can't stand at it.

Villager 1 : No one can. But in emergency, you have to. Really, we do not know what is in store for us. Just take a look all around.

Villager 2: Patients are suffering from various diseases. There's a heart breaking scenario all around.

Villager 1 : It seems the condition of some of them is improving, whereas that of others is deteriorating.

Villager 2 : You're right. Some seem to be hovering between life and death.

Villager 1 : Come on this way. This is ward number one. Look! A patient is tossing on the bed. He has stomach-ache. The other has clutched his head with both his hands. His head is perhaps reeling.

Villager 2 : Very dreadful! The third patient over there in the corner is spitting blood. The fourth one is in a coma.

Villager 1 : Dr. Dwivedi is on the round. We should call him back to attend the patient.

Villager 2 : No. It's not your job. The doctor knows all about. Let's move on.

Villager 1 : Lo! It's ward number thirteen. There's a cancer patient crying with pain.

Villager 2: He seems to be counting the last moments of his life. O my God! He has breathed his last. What do you Think of all this?

Villager 1 : We think that hospital is a place where one can see the spectacle of meeting and parting.
Villager 2 : You are right. Let's move out. I just can't stand this sight.
Villager 1 : Ok. Let's be on our way...

25. IMPORTANCE OF HEALTH

(Two intelligent students are talking about the importance of good health. Let's see as to what way they talk in.)

Philip : Hello, Joseph! How are you?

Joseph : Fine. And you?

Philip : Very well. Do you know there's an essay competition in our school on the importance of good health.

Joseph : Well, I have been on leave for three days. Nice to know this from you. What do you think on the topic?

Philip : Well, I think that health is a priceless wealth. It is impossible to purchase health with money.

Joseph : Also, a healthy body has a healthy mind—people say so.

Philip : Truly said. The mental condition of an unhealthy fellow deteriorates. You will find a healthy fellow always happy.

Joseph : Yes, I agree with you. An unhealthy fellow is always sad and worried. Cleanliness is as important for health as nutritious diet.

Philip : Not only this, but bodily cleanliness, clean house, pure water and fresh air are also very necessary.

Joseph : Yes, you are correct. Besides, the diet should be delicious, digestive and nutritious, shouldn't it?

Philip : Surely. Our teacher often used to say that physical Exercise and recreation are also necessary for health. In fact, sound health is the be-all and end-all of life.

Joseph : And much on this is that a person who is infirm, sick

and unhealthy is a burden for his family.
Philip : You are a good friend. Always agree to a certain point.
Joseph : Thanks for your intelligent thoughts. Bye!
Philip : Bye!

26. CONVERSATION BETWEEN TRAIN PASSENGERS
(Two passengers are talking in the waiting hall.)
Passenger 1 : Yeah, this is the Patna Junction Railway Station.
Passenger 2 : What a rush! A lot of hue and cry. The platform is packed to its capacity.
Passenger 1: There's a great rush these days. Have you come from Mumbai and waiting for someone dear to you?
Passenger 2 : Yes, I have come from Mumbai and waiting for my driver to come.
Passenger 1 : Well, the down train from Mumbai has just passed. So, I thought you might have got down from that train and waiting for someone.
Passenger 2 : Ok, you are right. Well, what are you waiting for?
Passenger 1 : I have to go to Rewa. Waiting for the Pawan Express.
Passenger 2 : But the Pawan Express does not go to Rewa. It is direct via Satna.

Passenger 1 : Yes, you are right. But I will get down at Satna and move onward by bus or by local train.
Passenger 2 : Good idea.
Passenger 1 : There's a heavy crowd of people at the booking counter. The pick pockets have a field day.
Passenger 2 : You are right. I've also been a victim of a pick-pocket last year. There's a big chance of pick pocketing at such places.
Passenger 1 : Not only this. The hawkers are also making brisk business. They are growing restive for grabbing undue money.
Passenger 2 : Lo! The train has come. There's a commotion all

around. The passengers surge forward. Oh! It is very difficult to board the train. Anyhow...

(Passenger 2 moves towards the train and enters it.)
Passenger 2 : Is this the 2nd sleeper?
Passenger 3 : Yes, it is. What's your berth number?
Passenger 2 : It is 22. That one. The side upper.
Passenger 3 : Good. The train steams off at the right time.
Passenger 2 : Is this the Satna Station?
Passenger 3 : Yes, it is. Do hurry to get it down. The train is standing for quite a long time.
Passenger 2 : Oh! I must hurry...Thanks for your cooperation.
Passenger 3 : Thanks and bye!

27. IN A RESTAURANT

(Madhav and Ashita alongwith their son, Ojas, go to a restaurant to have lunch. See how they converse with the waiter.)

Ashita : How about a cup of tea?

Madhav : No, not at home. I wish to go to a good restaurant today.

Ashita : Good idea. It has been a long time since we visited any restaurant. So let's go.

Ojas : What a pleasant idea, Mom!

Madhav : So let's get ready and move quickly.

(They reached the restaurant.)

Ojas : Can you serve me orange juice?

Waiter : Yes, all available here.

Ojas : Please fetch it to me.

Waiter : OK. Just serving...

Ashita : Can we have the menu, please?

Ashita : Will you have soup?

Madhav : Yes, tomato soup.

Ashita : Tomato soup for two.

Ojas : And a cheese sandwich for me.

Waiter : Yes, serving. What would you like for your main course?

Madhav : I'd have fried rice and some vegetable with potato and cauliflower.

Ashita : The same for us. What more vegetables do you have?

Waiter : We've potato curry, brinjal-bari and palak-paneer, madam.

Ashita : Give me palak-paneer.

Waiter : Do you want coffee at the end?

Ashita : No, not coffee. We'll take ice-cream.

Madhav : Three scoops of Vanilla ice-cream.

Waiter : Here...
Ashita : What's the bill for?
Waiter : It's for only Rs. 360/-, madam.
Madhav : Here's the money.
Waiter : Thanks. Visit again, sir.

28. QUESTIONS DURING INTERVIEW
Part-I
Question: What is your name?
Answer : My name is Ritesh.
Question: What are your subjects?
Answer: My subjects are Physics, Chemistry and
Biology.
Question: How did you do in the exam?
Answer: Very well. I hope to pass in the first
division.
Question: What do you propose to do after the result
is announced?
Answer : I want to sit for the Medical Test
Examination.
Question: Oh! Are you going to be a doctor?
Answer: Yes, of course. It is no lukewarm desire; it is
a red hot purpose.

Question: Why do you want to be a doctor?
    Answer: It is a noble profession. Besides, it provides ample scope for
selfless service, doesn't it?
    Question: But what about those doctors who trade in
human misery?
    Answer: They're social parasites, a slur on the fair
name of this noble profession.
    Question: How can you uphold the honour of your profession?
    Answer: I shall try to live up to its high ideals.
    Question: Brave words. But will you act what you
preach?
    Answer: The proof of the pudding is in the eating.
    Interviewer: That'll do. You may go.

ART OF CONVERSATION: EASY TO LEARN

Part-II

Question: Is your name Ravindra?

Answer: Yes, sir.

Question: What did you take this morning?

Answer: I took two slices of bread, a little butter and a cup of milk.

Question: Did two slices satisfy your hunger?

Answer: I'm not glutton. What matters is quality, and not quantity.

Question: Are you a vegetarian or a non-vegetarian?

Answer : I'm a non-vegetarian.

Question: What do you prefer- meat or fish?

Answer : I have special liking for fishes. They're so delicious.

Question: What is the secret of your robust health?

Answer: I exercise regularly. And I go for a walk early in the morning. It does me a lot of good.

Question: How?

Answer: What a delight it is to see Nature bathed in the morning sunshine! It lifts up the spirit.

Question: But how do you leave your bed on a cold wintry morning?

Answer : Minor discomforts stand nowhere in comparison to greater gain. Besides, there is such a thing as the force of habit.

29. QUESTIONS ON ENERGY CONSERVATION

(Some students are asking questions to their teacher on energy conservation. See how the students are asking questions and the teacher is answering all them.)

Students : Good morning, sir.

Teacher : Good morning.

Students : Well, we have to learn today about energy conservation.

Teacher : It's a very good topic. Just come on the subject and ask your questions.

Student 1 : Well, what's the meaning of energy?

Teacher : Students, take care. Energy means the ability to put effort and enthusiasm into an activity, work, etc.

For example- "It is a waste of time and energy."

Student 2 : And what about conservation?

Teacher 1 : The root word is conserve. It means to use as little of something as possible so that it lasts a long time.

It also means to protect something and prevent it from being changed or destroyed. And the course of

action is called conservation. As for example- wild life conservation, environment conservation, etc.

Student 3 : Sir, how many types of source of energy are there?

Teacher : There are two types of source of energy-conventional and non-conventional. Coal, petroleum and firewood are conventional source of energy whereas water, wind, sun and bio-mass are non-conventional source of energy.

Student 4 : Define the traits of the two types of energy.

Teacher : Well, sources of conventional energy pollute the air.

They are limited. They will exhaust within a certain
period. Non-conventional energy are natural gifts.
They do not exhaust. They even do not pollute our
environment. They are free of cost.
Student 5 : That's right, sir. Why is it necessary to conserve it?
Teacher : Because it is limited. It is likely to last within a
certain period. We know our coal deposits are
supposed to last for around 100years. Oil and gas
reserves are also estimated to last for a limited
period only. So, it is necessary to consume it wisely
and conserve it for future use.
Student 6 : How to tackle energy crisis?
Teacher : The solar system should be tapped to electrify
houses and streets. It is cost effective. See-waves
and winds are also to be tapped to provide energy.
Hydro-electric power projects should be set in. This
will tackle energy crisis.
Students : Thank you, teacher.
Teacher : Thanks.

30. TALKING TO A FOREIGNER

(Federer, an American, visits India and meets Mr. Mihir Sen at India Gate, New Delhi. See how they talk.)
Stranger : Hello, my friend! What's your name and where've

you come from?

Federer : I'm Federer, an American. I've come from New York. Your good name, please?
Stranger : I'm Mihir Sen, a social activist.
Federer : Good. Please tell me about this monument. What is it

about?

Mihir : This is India Gate, a historic monument. It has been

built in the memory of the martyrs of the Second World War. Look at the names of the soldiers who died for the sake of the nation. They were great warriors.

Federer : When was it built?
Mihir : It was built in 1947 by the Government of India.
Federer : Ok. I see. Other historic places at New Delhi?
Mihir : The Red Fort, The Janter Manter, the Qutub Minar,

the Mughal Garden, etc. Are you alone or with
family?

Federer : I'm with my wife, Mary and daughter, Yumiko.
Mihir : Good. Very good. How long do you have to stay at New Delhi?

Federer : I'm here for only two days.
Mihir : Then, better to hire a taxi and move all around. Don't

forget to visit the Science City, the Janter Manter and the National Museum.

Federer : Where's the most charming shopping centre?
Mihir : You may visit the Chandani Chowk.
Federer : Is there any park around here?
Mihir : Of course. You may enjoy the Green Park, a little

ahead the Ring Road.

Federer : Thanks for your kind information. Indians are

cooperative by their nature. Love to India and regards to the Indians.

Mihir : Thank you.

31. EMPLOYEE ON A FOREIGN TOUR

(Ronaldo has been selected for official tour to Australia and New Zealand. See how he talks with his boss and other friend.)

Neymar : Hello, Ronaldo! There's a good news for you.

Ronaldo : Hello, just tell me. What is it?

Neymar : Well, the boss has selected you for the next tour to Australia. Your tour will commence on first of the month. It is a ten-day tour. Your wife is allowed to accompany you.

Ronaldo : Thanks to God! It is very surprising for us. But are

you sure? I have a doubt over it.

Neymar : Really, it is. I am your best friend. I never pass false information. I can't do so.

Ronaldo : Thanks for the information. I may meet my boss and

express my gratitude.

(Ronaldo goes to his boss to express his feeling.)

Ronaldo : Thank you, sir. You have bestowed faith onto me.

Always appraised my work. My wife is very happy to know this.

Boss : It is my duty to take care of my employees and encourage them to work better. You had always done

good and worked in the interest of the company. You have made much profit to the company. So, I selected you this time.

Ronaldo : We have already purchased two tickets. My wife has made all preparations. We would fly to a foreign country for the first time. We would stay in Alphones Arena in Sydney. We'll enjoy local sightseeing. We'll visit Art Gallery, zoos, gardens, etc. We would also move to Auckland in New Zealand. There's a Campwell Samadhi.

Boss : It is a good planning. Do not forget to see Sky-Tower in Auckland. It is situated at the corner of Federal and Victoria streets. At night, it shines like the Taj in India.

Ronaldo : And for Melbourne, sir. Any idea?
Boss : Melbourne is a big city in Australia. It's very

attractive.

Ronaldo : Nice sir.
Boss : With best wishes. Happy journey.

32. RECORDING OF A MUSIC PROGRAMME

(An Artiste visits Doordarshan Kendra for recording of her music. See how she talks with the producer.)

Artiste : This is Doordarshan Kendra, I see. Is there any programme production from this Kendra?

S/Guard : Yes, you are right. There's. But what's your purpose?

Artiste : Well, I am a musician. I can sing, dance and even play the flute. I want to present a debut at this Kendra.

S/Guard : OK. You may talk to the receptionist sitting over

there.

Artiste : Good morning, sir. I am a musician and want to meet Music Director for recording of my programme.

Receptionist: Good morning, madam. Nice to see you. Please write

Here your name and full address. Please go straightway. Take a little turn to right and you will be there at studio building.

Artiste : Thank you.

(The Artiste goes to the Studio building and meets Music Director.)

Artiste : Good morning, sir. I am Kavita. I sing

melodiously; dance well; and even play the flute. I want to exhibit my art.

Music Director: Just start. Go on in your full swing.

Artiste : Singing... Playing music...

Music Director: Very well. We will record your song. It'd be a nice presentation. Your programme is to be recorded on

Monday next week. This will be telecast the same day and will be followed subsequent three days.

Artiste : Thank you, sir. But what would be the artiste fee?

Music Director : For your fee, contact Programme Secretary sitting in that room.

Artiste : My music programme is scheduled to be recorded.

What would be the fee to be paid to me?

Prog. Secy. : Let me prepare your contract paper. Your fee would stand at Rs. 2000/- for a single recording of fifteen minutes. Please put your signature here.
Artiste : Thank you, sir.
Prog. Secy. : Thanks.

33. VOCATIONAL TRAINING

(Some students of Journalism and Mass Communication approach Doordarshan Kendra and request for vocational training for one month. Go through the conversation they talk to one another.)

Student : We are students of Journalism and Mass
Communication. Want to meet the Head of Office for
training purpose.

Receptionist: Yes, of course. You may meet but where have you
come from?

Student : We all are of the same college i.e. L S College at
location. We have completed three years Degree course
in Journalism and Mass Communication. We have come
for vocational training.

Receptionist: Please show me your identity cards and write all your
names and mobile Nos. I will take you to the Director
of the Kendra.

Student : Here they are.

Receptionist: Sitting in the Chamber is the Director of the Kendra.
You may meet him. But you should first meet his PA,
Mr. Manish, sitting in that room.

Student : OK. Thank you.

(In the PA room.)

Student : Good morning, Sir. We want to meet the Director.
Could you please help us?

PA : Yes, surely. Our boss is in. But he is a bit busy. You
can't meet him this time. Just wait for half an hour
or come again at 2.30 pm.

Student : Better to wait for half an hour.

PA : But what's the work with you?

Student : Just for vocational training in journalism we have
come.

PA : Good idea. Follow me. I'll get you to our boss. He'll allow your training in this campus. You'll have to deposit a DD for Rs. 500/- as fee for the training.

Student : OK, sir. Here's the DD for Rs. 500/- in the name of your DDO.

Director : You all are good students. You are allowed for one month vocational training in this Kendra. Our seven experts will teach and guide you in different fields. Just follow them. Ask maximum questions. Don't hesitate at all. Classes will run from 10.30am to 04.30 pm every day except closed holidays. Take care and learn a lot. That's all.

Students : Thank you, sir.

34. VISIT TO A RADIO STATION

(Dr. Chandra, a Senior Journalist, visits a Radio Station. See how he talks with staff members thereat.)

Security Guard: Good morning, sir. May I know who you are and where do you come from?

Dr. Chandra : I'm Dr. Chandra, a free-lance Journalist. I've come to see you all.

Security Guard: Yeah. Just come on, sir. This is All India Radio, a Government in India. Please meet our receptionist.
She will accompany you up to theDy. Director of
this Station.

Dr. Chandra : Good afternoon, madam. I'm a free-lance
journalist. I want to meet the General Manager of this
station..

Receptionist : Good afternoon, sir. We're here to receive you.
Please come along. I may get you in touch with Dr.
Mitra, Dy. Director of this Station.

(Dr. Chandra meets Dr. Mitra, Dy. Director, who takes him up to all sections of the Station.)

Dy. Director: This is our Administrative Block. They're all
Ministerial Staff. They hold the posts like LDC, UDC,
Accountant and Cashier.

Dr. Chandra: Good. They're smart personnel.

Dy. Director: This is our Programme Section. Total twenty
Employeesare there.They're Transmission
Executive, Programme Producer, Script Writer,
Voice Recorder, Studio Attendant, etc.

Dr. Chandra: Very well. And where is the Studio?

Dy. Director: Here is. We record our special programme in Studio.
That's the News Room.

Dr. Chandra: Quite exciting. Is there any live Studio transmission?

Dy. Director: Yes. There is. There's live transmission from our studio on every Tuesday. We often call for a doctor to answer live the general public on certain specific issue of general importance.

Dr. Chandra: Marvellous. Great achievement!

Dy.Director: She's our newly recruited Programme Officer. She's very sincere. She's recently produced a tele-film "Nari-Shakti" on women empowerment.

Dr. Chandra: Yeah, we see. Its theme is quite appreciative. It's the need of the hour and demand of time. Good production. I would like to request you to repeat its transmission in the near future.

Dy. Director: Certainly. We'll do this on Thursday. Let's move to the transmission building.

Dr. Chandra: Is this the transmission tower?

Dy. Director: Yes, this is the.

Dr. Chandra: What height it might be?

Dy. Director: It is 100 metre tall, a little less or a little more.

Dr. Chandra: And the transmission machinery?

Dy. Director: Here they're. This one is for national broadcast and that one is for FM Channel.

Dr. Chandra: Surprising. Really, our country has made much miracle in the field of science and technology. It has been a long time here... I have to be back. Nice to see you all. Thanks for your co-operation.

Dy. Director: Thanks.

35. A CRICKET MATCH

(Vini and Rubel are watching a cricket match with their uncle. Let's see how they talk with one another.)

Vini : What's your plan? How to enjoy the vacation?

Rubel : Nothing is. I'm getting bored.

Vini : The same is here. I think, tomorrow's the final match of IPL 8. Let's go and enjoy.

Rubel: Surely. The match is between Mumbai Indians and Chennai Superkings in our city itself. It'd be a keenly contested

match. Who do you support?

Vini : Mumbai Indians is my favourite. And yours?

Rubel : I'm a big fan of Dhoni. He's a very good player. And a captain of CSK as well. So, I wish Chennai to win this

season.

Vini : I've got two tickets. One is for you. Take this.

Rubel : Thank you. Let's meet at 7.30 pm tomorrow at Eden Gardens.

Vini : OK. Bye!

(Rubel and Vini are proceeding to the stadium with their uncle.)

Rubel : Let's go fast. I think the match has started.

Vini : It's likely to start. Lo! the CSK has won the toss and opted to bowl first.

Uncle : Do you want some juice or pop-corns?

Rubel : Surely, I do want so.

Uncle : Take this. The game has begun and the players are on the ground.

Vini : See Rohit and Simmons on the ground. They're playing a dashing game right from the beginning. They've shattered the opponents.

Rubel : Rayudu and Pollard hit some meaty blows in the end to help

MI to a huge score. I think CSK will chase this one and win.

Uncle : It's a brief break now. Take some ice-cream and pastries. The game will start again in a few minutes. CSK is unable to get off a good start. Bowlers of Mumbai are doing a good job. Harbhajan took the wickets of Smith and Raina. See Dhoni is out by Malinga.

Rubel : With four overs remaining, CSK need 78 runs to win. It's a very tough competition. Celebrations are already in progress for Mumbai Indians.

Vini : Yes, MI managed to stave off CSK by 41 runs and claim their 2nd IPL title.

Rubel : Who is the man of the match?

Vini : The captain himself is the man of the match. It's Rohit Sharma.

Rubel : It was a very challenging match but MI won.

Vini : I enjoyed the match very much.

Rubel : But, I am very disappointed seeing CSK's performance. They played very badly.

Uncle : No matter. It was a game played with a sense of game itself. Either one team has to test defeat. It's very late now. Let's hurry home.

36. TALK ON THE FUTURE OF CHILDREN

(Given below are conversations between the teacher, guardian and student. Learn how they make a good talk.)

Teacher : Today is the 14th November, the Children's Day. What do you know all about?

Student : Sir, it is the birthday of Pt. Jawahar Lal Nehru, the first Prime Minister of India. He had deep love for the children. So, his birthday is celebrated as the Children's Day.

Teacher : What do you think about the children's future of India?

Guardian : Good subject... On the subject, I think that the progress of a country depends on the children, isn't it?

Teacher : Yeah, they are the future of India, aren't they?

Guardian : I think. It is necessary that they are properly looked after. They should be provided proper facilities for their education.

Teacher : Certainly from their very childhood. A child feels an urge to do many things. He then needs good caring and heavy support from his guardians. And in some ways, from his teachers also. Some want to be painters and some lawyers or doctors. But their parents kill their inner urge and cast them into their own mould.

Guardian: You are right, sir. Some guardians do so, but not all. Such children fail to do any good to the society or for the country in future. But what do you think is the reason behind it, sir.

Teacher : In our country some superstitious customs have been coming down for ages. It is not so with the other countries of the world. In those countries the natural aptitude of children is given due weight.

Guardian: Yes. I agree with you. We crush their curiosity. In other countries, there is not as such. We, the parents, should think that our children should be

encouraged and given opportunity to their tastes.

Teacher : That's right, sir. We should try to do our best.

37. TOWN LIFE AND VILLAGE LIFE

(Given below are the merits and demerits of town life and village life. See how the two people talk.)

Nitin : Good morning, Jitin. Seeing you after ages! Where had you been?

Jitin : Good morning. I had been to my village.

Nitin : How do you manage to stand the boredom of village life? To me, it is a veritable drudgery.

Jitin : Quite unfortunate indeed for you to have developed a distaste for village life. Don't you feel an urge to get away from the cramped atmosphere of towns and be in communion with Nature.

Nitin : But how long can Nature keep us engaged? Natural beauties are meant only for those who can see them. To me, village life seems to be highly monotonous. There is a little scope for variety, isn't it? And variety is the spice of life.

Jitin : But I am sure a man doesn't want only variety to live upon, does he ? What are these blessed varieties brought upon us— hurry, worry, obsessions and hell.

Nitin : Don't be a fool, Jitin. You seem to have developed an escapist tendency. I admit that town life is beset with problems. But we have to fight them through and not to run away from them.

Jitin : Again one of your usual digressions. Why do you equate a longing for country life with escapism?

Nitin : Because you cannot display your talents
among village folk. They are so very
illiterate and superstitious, aren't they?
Their silly arguments often tease you out of
thought.

Jitin : I'm afraid you are becoming too harsh.
Don't you realize that India is essentially a
country of villages. We can't progress by
neglecting them. I would rather advise you
to go to your village and do all that you can
to modernize it.

Nitin : Enough of your moral teaching. Let us for
the time being agree to disagree. Good-bye!

38. CINEMA-ADDICT AND CINEMA-HATER

(Here's a dialogue between a cinema-addict and a cinema-hater. See how they talk.)

Anil : Good afternoon, Sunil. I have come to drag you out of your house.

Sunil : But why? You seem to be in your elements.

Anil : Yes. Haven't you read today's paper? *Pakeeza* has been released.

Sunil : From what jail?

Anil : By God, what a moron you are! Haven't you heard the name of *Pakeeza*? Come on. Hurry up. I have already bought two tickets.

Sunil : Don't be a dandy. I don't understand why you have become so mad after films.

Anil : Don't be an old-timer. This film is a fine musical hit.

Sunil : Why not? Every hero and heroine of Indian films is supposed to be a singer. What nonsense! Do you think these films are in any way connected with real life? What do you find in them? —a boy-meets-a-girl theme, love at first sight, a villain making abusive dialogue, etc.

Anil : Yours is nothing but a jaundiced view. Why do you want films to be realistic? They are for our entertainment.

Sunil : Of course, they are. But are they not corroding the moral basis of our society? Don't you see our youngsters are being spoiled? All their time is wasted in slavish imitation of their favourite stars.

Anil : I am not at all in a mood to quarrel with you

on this point. But I am quite sure your opinion is lopsided. Have you watched the film *Life's Good* released recently?

Sunil : No, I haven't watched any of such films, nor do I wish to watch them.

39. STORY OF A TRAVEL-WEARY

(Aalia is telling a story to Sajia on the journey of a traveller. See how the two friends go with the story.)

Sajia : Hello, Aalia! Where had you been? Have met after a long time.

Aalia : I had been to my native village. It was summer vacation. So, my dad took me to village. Returned yesterday only.

Sajia : How did it remain all this?

Aalia : All usual. Nothing special. There was scorching heat. However, we moved to our countryside. Though, it was not the proper time. During the journey, we saw a travel-weary. There's a story. Nothing to say about him.

Sajia : But what's the story. Just tell me.

Aalia : It was the month of June; the scorching heat. A Traveller was travel-weary.

Sajia : Ok! Just go with the story.

Aalia : Surely. His destination was away, far away. There was no water all around. He was down with thirst.

Sajia : Was there no oasis?

Aalia : No, nothing like that. The traveller became sad. His heart began to sink. He closed his eyes.

Sajia : Hadn't you helped him in a way?

Aalia : Certainly, but he didn't take it. He, nevertheless, continued his march on.

Sajia : What happened then?

Aalia : Then, the song of a nightingale lifted up his dropping spirit. Tears welled up in his eyes. As he was thirsty, I gave him water. He drank it to his satisfaction.

Sajia : Next?
Aalia : Then, he rested for a while. After having been refreshed, he returned to his journey.
Sajia : It might be a pitiable scene. May God help such people!

1. TRIAL IN THE COURT OF VENICE

(Here's the trial of a case against Antonio, the merchant of Venice, filed by Shylock, the money lender. Let's see how the trial goes.)

Portia : Antonio, I've studied the entire case filed against you.

Antonio : Ok, Madam. Well, I could not repay the money within three months, and as per the Bond I have to

give Shylock one pound of flesh from my body... O my God! What an ill fate of mine! Hope, you could do a little for me.

Portia : Nothing to worry, Antonio. God stands with the weak but the honest. Law is with you. Don't get

disheartened.

(Trial begins in the Court of Venice.)
Portia : Lo! The court begins. Just come on.
Antonio : Your majesty, Me Lord.
Justice : You are accused of not repaying the money as per the agreement. What have you to say against all this?
Antonia : I beg pardon for delay of payment. My lawyer Would stand against the case on my behalf.
Portia : Me Lord. Antonio is a small merchant. He has suffered a heavy loss in his business during last one year. Hence, he couldn't repay in time. But in a few days to come, he'll surely. Pray your high gesture to extend life to him by not taking a pound of flesh from his body.

Shylock : The bond doesn't favour Antonio. I must take a pound of flesh from his body.

Portia : But if it's allowed, he'll die.

Shylock : Justice is justice. It doesn't bother who dies or who survives.

Portia : It won't be a justice of any kind. Justice is to support life and to allow survival.

Shylock : I want nothing but a pound of flesh, Me Lord.

Portia : Ok. He be allowed Me Lord! But without shedding

any drop of blood as this bond does not allow shedding blood anyway.

Justice : Mr. Shylock, what you want is to take the life of

Antonio that law does not allow. Your Bond has been executed against the rules of Natural Justice. It stands vitiated. You have lost your case. You are even not allowed to get your principal money. Case is dismissed.

Portia : Thanks for justice, Me Lord!